ULT

PUPPY
TRAINING
FOR
BEGINNERS

4 BOOKS IN 1

Train Your Dream Pooch in Just 4 Weeks!

Charlotte Marley

Amazing Bonuses

Inside the book
Scroll to the end
and scan the QR
Code

Table of content

1.   **Small Breed Adult Dog (For example: Chihuahua)**
2.   **Large Breed Puppy (For example:Labrador Retriever)**
3.   **Senior Dog (For example:German Shepherd)**

House Training
Basics of House Training
Setting a Routine
Reinforcing Positive Behaviors

Prevention and Correctionof Behavioral Issues

UNDERSTANDINGDOG MENTAL HEALTH & STIMULATION

Identifying Your Dog'sMental Needs

Problem-Solving Games

Sensory Engagement Activities

Quick and Fun MentalStimulation

ADVANCED MENTALEXERCISES

Advanced Problem-SolvingActivities

Skill-Enhancing Games

INTRODUCTION

Embark on a transformative journey with the "Ultimate Puppy Training for Beginners," a comprehensive guide designed to deepen the bond between you and your cherished canine companion. This guide, penned by renowned canine expert Charlotte Marley, stands as a testament to her two decades of experience in dog behavior and training. A respected figure in canine behavioral science, Marley presents her innovative approach that seamlessly merges positive reinforcement with psycho-attitudinal balance, revolutionizing the dynamics of human-canine relationships.

Throughout her esteemed career, Marley's insights have enriched numerous dogs and their owners, fostering mutual understanding, happiness, and improved quality of life. The "Dog Training Bible" epitomizes her dedication, serving both newcomers to dog ownership and seasoned handlers alike.

This book transcends being just a guide. It is your gateway to deeply understanding your dog's mind, fostering an unbreakable bond, and cherishing the profound love and respect inherent in the human-canine bond. Dive into this enlightening journey, with Charlotte Marley at the helm, and discover the transformative power of the positive reinforcement techniques, infusing your life with harmony and an unmatched connection with your furry friend.

As we embark on this captivating journey, I'm reminded of the words of esteemed veterinarian and author, Nicholas H. Dodman: *"Dogs are humanity's closest allies. Understanding them better is the least we owe them."*

Enjoy your reading journey!

As an independent author, your feedback means the world to me.

Would you mind leaving an honest review on Amazon? It helps immensely and takes just a moment. Just scan the QR code or copy/paste this url:

https://www.amazon.com/review/create-review/?asin= B0CT5TK5JD

Essential checklist to train your Puppy

An essential checklist for training your puppy includes several items.

- First, you'll need a sturdy leash made of materials like nylon, leather, or heavy cotton. It's important to create a positive association between your dog and the leash, which can make going for walks or car rides easier. Reward your dog with training treats when you clip the leash to their harness. Treats can also be helpful in redirecting their attention if they tend to chew on the leash. Even if you have a secure property, leash training is necessary for vet visits and public spaces.

- Next, consider a flat-buckle or breakaway collar for your dog. Collars are useful for carrying identification and other necessary documents, but it's generally better to attach the leash to a harness rather than the collar. Collars should be loose enough to fit two fingers between the collar and your dog's skin to avoid strain or chafing. A collar alone is not sufficient for controlling or restraining your dog during walks.

- A properly-fitted front-clip harness is recommended for general activities such as walks and car rides. However, it should be taken off during playtime with other dogs or while in the house to prevent accidents. Improperly fitted harnesses or excessive wear can cause discomfort or even gait issues. Despite the debate, harnesses are still a safer option than leashes for restraining dogs, as they eliminate the risk of neck damage.

- Using a training clicker is a personal choice, but it can aid in teaching your dog various behaviors. Clickers are inexpensive and can be found at pet supply stores or online. Alternatively, you can use any household object that produces a distinct clicking noise. The key is to develop a positive association with the sound for effective training.

- Delicious dog treats are essential for motivating and rewarding your dog during training exercises. Choose low-calorie, high-reward treats that your dog finds enticing. A successful training program requires a generous amount of treats, so it's important to find affordable, portable options that won't contribute to weight gain. Boiled chicken is a recommended training treat, but you can also consider using vegetables if your dog enjoys them.

Finally, it's crucial to avoid using certain training tools that can cause harm to your dog. These include choke collars, prong collars, head halters, and electric shock systems. Opt for positive reinforcement methods instead. I've found that regularly assessing and updating your puppy's equipment is crucial to ensuring their needs are being met as they grow. As puppies grow quickly, it's important to make sure their equipment, such as their collar and leash, fit properly and are appropriate for their size and activity level. Additionally, as their needs change, such as if they become more active or require different types of toys, it's important to update their equipment accordingly. By doing so, you can help keep your puppy safe, healthy, and happy.

PUPPY TRAINING

"Once you have had a wonderful dog, a life without one, is a life diminished."

—Dean Koontz

Understanding Your Puppy's Growth Stages

Young puppies can bring both excitement and challenges to new dog owners and their furry friends. Like children puppies go through different stages of growth and development each with its own set of milestones and expectations. Understanding these developmental phases is crucial in meeting your puppy's physical, mental, and emotional needs.

Key Developmental Milestones

Being aware of the key developmental milestones in your puppy's' life is essential as it helps you determine when to introduce specific training and socialization activities. Lets' take a closer look at these milestones:

- **Neonatal period (0-2 weeks):** During this stage puppies rely completely on their mother for warmth, nourishment, and stimulation. Their eyes and ears are still closed. So they primarily rely on their sense of touch and smell to explore the world around them.

- **Transitional period (2-4 weeks):** At this stage puppies begin to venture out into their surroundings. Their eyes and ears open up allowing them to start interacting with their littermates. They also start developing motor skills, which enables them to move around more confidently.

- **Socialization period (4-14 weeks):** This phase is incredibly important as it is when puppies are most open to new experiences. It's the perfect time to introduce them to various people, animals, and environments. During this period they learn how to communicate with other dogs and humans while also grasping basic commands.

- **Juvenile period (14 weeks-6 months):** As puppies enter this stage they become more independent and curious about the world around them. It's a crucial time for continued learning and refinement of social skills. Enrolling in a puppy training class can help reinforce good behavior while addressing any unwanted ones.

- **Adolescence (6-18 months):** During adolescence puppies undergo hormonal changes that may lead to increased energy levels or occasional stubbornness while testing boundaries. Consistent training is vital during this phase along with providing appropriate outlets for both physical and mental stimulation.

By understanding these key developmental milestones. You can ensure that you are providing the necessary support and guidance for your puppy's overall well-being.

What to Expect at Various Ages

Understanding the different stages of your poppy's growth can greatly aid you in customizing your approach to training them while offering the necessary support for their overall well-being.

When they are between 8 12 weeks old is the ideal time for acquainting them with their new living environment as well as teaching them essential commands like "sit", "stay," and "come" using encouraging methods of reinforcement. It is also advisable to commence house training routines along with crate training during this phase. Between 12 16 weeks old is another crucial period that calls for reinforcing the basic commands already covered. Furthermore. It is important to progressively introduce new commands during this time. Prioritize their socialization by exposing them to an array of different sights, sounds, and environments. Additionally, it is a good time to initiate leash training while encouraging appropriate chewing habits with the help of suitable toys. Once your puppy reaches 4 6 months old and energy levels start to rise. It becomes even more vital to ensure they receive appropriate exercise and playtime as they grow.

You will be better prepared to give your puppy the essential training, socialization, and support they require to grow into a well-rounded, self-assured adult dog if you are aware of their growth stages and developmental milestones. Having a successful and joyful puppyhood requires patience, persistence, and a positive outlook.

Gradually introduce more advanced commands while simultaneously working on strengthening their recall skills. While accidents may still happen during house training at this stage. Patience and consistency are key attributes to maintain during this process. Between 6 12 months old. Some adolescent behaviors may start surfacing as your puppy tests boundaries and your patience. To successfully navigate through this phase. Strive for consistency in training methods. Employ positive reinforcement techniques consistently. And maintain a well-structured routine for them. By acknowledging their growth stages along with their accompanying developmental milestones.

You will be better equipped in providing the essential training. Proper socialization experiences, and necessary support required for them to grow into confident and well-rounded adult dogs. A patient demeanor coupled with persistence and a positive outlook greatly contribute towards a successful and joyous journey through the puppyhood phase.

Age-Appropriate Training for Your Puppy

It is extremely important that you train your puppy to ensure that you have a well behaved and well-adjusted furry companion. However. It is vital to remember that your training approach should be tailored to your poppy's age and stage of development. This section will present you with age-appropriate training methods and exercises specifically designed to help your puppy succeed.

8-12 weeks

During a period ranging from 8-12 weeks old, your beloved young furry companion exhibits tremendous enthusiasm towards learning while remaining highly receptive towards new experiences encountered along the way. It becomes an opportune moment when one can introduce certain basic obedience commands crucial for establishing a strong foundation essential for future training endeavors ahead.

Presently, it proves exceedingly advantageous to engage in crate training techniques that allow gradual familiarity with designated spaces whilst imparting utmost comfort within them. Increasing time confinement helps instill feelings of security thereby creating favorable perceptions associated with the crate. Similarly, at this juncture, house training initiatives can commence by establishing a consistent routine inclusive of specific intervals directing your puppy to definite areas designated for its personal relief.

Patience and consistency remain key factors wherein duly acknowledging and praising your puppy's successful outdoor bathroom efforts play an integral role. Moreover, now would present itself as an ideal moment to begin acquainting your young pup with primary commands encompassing "sit," "stay," and "come." Employing positive reinforcement through rewards such as treats and abundant praise facilitates effective acknowledgment of their dedicated commitment.

12-16 weeks

As your precious puppy grows into a well-round- ed adult canine companion it is imperative that you continue reinforcing the basic commands they have already mastered while simultaneously introducing new ones. Leash training plays an influential role in this progression - start by gradually acquainting them with the sensation of wearing a collar and being on a leash. Begin walking sessions in serene environments where distractions are minimal.

Offering praise generously when they exhibit calmness while walking alongside you. Nurturing their socialization skills is essential as well - exposing them regularly to diverse sights, sounds, and experiences will ensure their comfort in various situations later on. Facilitating opportunities for playdates with other furry friends and acquainting them lovingly with different types of individuals as well as animals will contribute positively to their growth.

Last but not least. Encourage proper chewing habits whilst curtailing any inappropriate tendencies through providing an assortment of suitable chew toys tailored specifically for their needs. Redirecting any wayward chewing behavior towards these designated toys contributes greatly to their overall happiness and satisfaction.

4-6 months

At this stage it is essential to prioritize your poppy's increasing energy levels and curiosity by providing both physical and mental stimulation. It is recommended to advance from basic commands and introduce more complex ones, such as "heel," "leave it " and "off." By practicing these commands in different environments, you can assist your puppy in generalizing the desired behaviors. Additionally. Focus on enhancing your puppy's recall skills by consistently practicing the "come" command within a safe and enclosed area. Gradually increase the level of distractions to make the training more challenging. Lastly. Make sure that your puppy gets enough daily exercise and playtime to help them release excess energy and prevent boredom related behaviors.

6-12 months

As your puppy enters adolescence, they may under- go hormonal changes that can sometimes result in boundary testing and occasional stubbornness. To assist your puppy in navigating through this challenging stage. It is essential to maintain consistency and structure by adhering to a regular training routine and structured schedule. Furthermore, ongoing socialization plays a crucial role in shaping your poppy's' behavior. Continuously expose them to new experiences and reinforce appropriate behaviors in different situations. In addition to this enrolling your puppy in an obedience or agility class can further refine their skills and offer them an extra source of mental stimulation.

Positive Training Methods for Puppy Training

Within the realm of puppy training, positive methodologies have experienced a notable rise in popularity owing to their high efficacy rates and compassionate foundations. By prioritizing reinforcement for desired behaviors, these techniques minimize dependence on punishments or coercive measures. This chapter delves into essential components that underpin positive approaches, providing guidance for successfully integrating them within your pup's individualized learning sessions.

Employing positive reinforcement techniques involves rewarding our delightful puppies with things they find pleasurable (like treats, praise or toys) as soon as they showcase desirable behavior. Such reinforcement assists in engraving in our puppies' minds that their actions bring about favorable consequences, which increases the likelihood that they will repeat these actions over time. For example, when teaching our young furry friends how to sit. It is crucial that we promptly provide them with a treat alongside some words of encouragement as soon as their adorable bottoms touch the ground. Eventually this association between sitting and receiving rewards results in heightened willingness on their part to comply when prompted. Timing becomes an essential factor while practicing positive reinforcement techniques along with consistent repetition. Ensuring that our puppies are rewarded immediately after displaying desired conduct enables them to form a clear link between their actions and the rewards they obtain. Repetition solidifies our puppies' grasp of command execution and expected behaviors.

By consistently practicing and reinforcing these behaviors. We bolster the efficacy of our training efforts. Thereby guaranteeing long term success. The choice of appropriate rewards also holds significant value within positive training methods. Opting for treats that hold considerable appeal for our puppies, such as small portions of cooked chicken or cheese. Often proves effective in capturing their undivided attention and motivating them to excel during training sessions. It is crucial to choose treats that can be easily consumed during these sessions so as not to leave our puppies feeling too full or uninterested prematurely. Furthermore, altering the types of treats we use can contribute towards keeping our furry friends fully engaged and stimulated throughout the entirety of their training sessions. Science based force free techniques form an integral part of positive reinforcement methods.

These techniques prioritize understanding natural behaviors exhibited by our little ones. As well as their individual learning processes. Rather than resorting to punishment or coercion. These methodologies focus on teaching through positive reinforcement instead.

Employing force free approaches generates a strong bond founded on trust between us and our adorable canine companions while preserving their emotional wellbeing throughout the entire training process. Utilizing clicker training, lure reward training and shaping are examples of scientific techniques that exclude any application of force in favor of positive reinforcement strategies. Encouraging your puppy to thinkand learn is vital. As it reinforces their natural desire to please you. An important part of positive training methods is effective communication with your furry friend. This means being able to interpret their body language and signals. While also using clear and consistent verbal and non-verbal cues during training sessions. To communicate effectively make sure to use the same commands and gestures for each behavior you are working on. And remember, being patient and observant will help you better understand your puppys' signals so that you can respond appropriately.

Crate Training

Crate training is an important aspect of puppy training that offers numerous benefits for both you and your beloved companion. It provides a safe and secure space for your puppy. Reducing the risk of accidents or injuries when you are unable to supervise them. Additionally, it can help expedite the house-training process by taking advantage of their natural instinct to keep their sleeping area clean. When traveling. A crate trained puppy will feel more comfortable and secure. Whether it's a short trip to the vet or a longer journey. Moreover. A crate can serve as a comforting "den" for your puppy. Reducing stress and anxiety in unfamiliar situations. To ensure a smooth introduction to the crate follow these steps:

1. Choose an appropriate crate that allows your puppy to stand up. Turn around. And lie down comfortably. Look for one with adjustable dividers so you can expand the space as your puppy grows.

2. Make the crate inviting by adding soft bedding, blankets, and some toys inside. Place it in a quiet area of your home where your puppy can feel relaxed.

3. Encourage your puppy to explore the crate by placing treats and toys inside. Initially leave the door open so they can come and go freely. Praise and reward them when they voluntarily enter the crate.

4. Gradually increase the time that the door is closed once your puppy is comfortable entering the crate. Start with just a few minutes and gradually

extend it over time. Remember to reward them with praise and treats for staying calm inside.

5. Start feeding your puppy meals inside the crate to further associate it with positive experiences.

Following these steps will help ensure that both you and your furry friend have a positive experience with crate training while maintaining their safety andwell-being. Establishing a positive correlation betweenyour puppy and their crate plays a vital role in ensur-ing their peace of mind when being confined. A useful approach involves crating them for short periods while you're home thereby avoiding an association between the crate and your absence. This practice aids in famil-iarizing them with the idea that regardless of proxim-ity. The crate serves as a secure haven where they can find comfort and relaxation overnight as well.

Potty Training

Let's paint a picture. There you are, in your living room, with an adorably mischievous puppy, new to your household and to the world. Lovable, yes, but he has one major flaw – he doesn't quite understand the concept of a toilet yet. He piddles and poops wherever his puppy instincts lead him, leaving behind not-so-adorable messes. Your precious carpets cry out, begging for mercy from the stinky onslaught. It's a mess! That's the problem, right? Your puppy needs potty training, not yesterday or tomorrow, but today. Step up, courageous pet parent! Here's your shield and sword – a guide to the battlefield.

Phase one, a schedule. Like clockwork, puppies. They are not much different from babies when it comes to this. They have tiny tummies, so they eat often and, well, what goes in must come out. Regular feeding times are a must. Set them, stick to them. Predictability is key. Trust me, it's easier for you too.

But how often should you let them out, you ask? Consider this - a three-month-old puppy can hold their bladder for about four hours. Age in months, that's their limit in hours. It's not a perfect rule, but it's a start. In doubt? Then go out!

Phase two is all about the training. Here's where we introduce the puppy to the great outdoors... or the designated indoor potty spot. Start by carrying them to the spot after meals and playtimes. And if they do their business there? Showers of praise. Treats too. Not too many though, remember those tiny tummies. However, not all goes according to plan. Accidents? They're going to happen. It's part of the process. When they do, keep your cool. Don't yell. No need to go all drill sergeant on the poor pup. Clean up the mess. Then, reinforce the correct behavior next time. No harm, no foul.

So, you may think, 'Wait, that's it?' Well, kinda, but there's a bit more. Patience. Consistency. These two are your silent warriors. Potty training won't happen overnight. Some days, it'll feel like your puppy is forgetting everything. But remember, Rome wasn't built in a day. And neither is a potty-trained puppy. The best part? It's all worth it. That first morning when you wake up to a clean carpet, the silent victory dance you'll do, priceless. Your little pup, growing up, learning new things. You're part of that journey. Every puddle, every little nugget is a step towards a clean, happy home.

And let's be honest, isn't that what we all want? A house that doesn't smell like a kennel, a puppy that's thriving, and that priceless bond that only grows stronger with every challenge you overcome together. That's the art of potty training. Simple steps, bit by bit, leading to big changes. So grab that leash and those biodegradable poop bags, let's get started, shall we?

Setting a Schedule

Imagine this – a meticulously set, tick-tocking schedule. A master plan to champion your puppy's pot- ty-training saga. Let's dive right in. First off, mornings. As soon as the first yawn escapes your sleepy pup, it's showtime. Out you go. The grass, the breeze, it's an al fresco bathroom experience. It sets the tone for the day. Meals. Your pup gulps down that kibble, slurps that water. Tummy full, the clock ticks. 15 to 30 minutes, no more, no less. Time for another trip outdoors. You see, digestion kicks in quickly for these little ones.

Nap times – they're sacred. Puppies snooze of- ten, recharging for their next adventure. But as soon as those eyes flutter open, it's elimination time once more. Swiftly, to the potty zone. Playtime ends and it's a straight shot to the potty spot. All that frolicking and chasing squeaky toys, it stirs up the urge, you see.

Finally, before the moon takes over the night shift, there's one last call for nature. Bedtime potty break. It's non-negotiable. Off to dreamland, bladder empty.

Young pups? They might need these potty rendez- vous every hour or two during daylight hours. But fret not, their bladder control betters with age. Soon, these frequent jaunts will taper off.

Okay, let's talk technique. Potty training's more marathon than sprint, you see. Patience, that's your secret weapon. And positive reinforcement, your golden ticket. Step one, the potty zone. Pick a spot. Any spot, but it's got to be consistent. This becomes their go-to toilet. Before long, they'll catch the drift. Step two, cue words. A phrase, a command. Maybe a "go potty" or "do your business". Use it when you're in the potty zone. They'll associate the words with the action in no time. Step three, the good stuff – praise and treats. As soon as the deed's done in the correct spot, make it rain affection. Treats too. They'll love it. It solidifies the link between the potty zone and the action. Step four, surveillance. Watch your pup like a hawk indoors. Sniffing, circling, whining? That's their tell. Outside, pronto. Nip those accidents in the bud.

Accidents? They're part of the journey. No puppy is perfect. Catch them in the act? A firm "no", then whisk them outdoors. If they finish up in the potty zone, bingo. Reinforcement achieved. Clean-up's crucial, though. Lingering scents could encourage repeat offenses. There you have it. Potty training 101. Sounds like a lot? Maybe. But once you get the hang of it, it'll be a breeze. And your carpets? They'll thank you.

Leash Training

Let's talk about leash training. It's not just a chore or a formality. No sirree, it's a skill. A skill every canine needs to master. Why, you ask? Well, my friend, it's about safety. It's about comfort. It's about making those walks and outdoor adventures a joy rather than a tug-o-war. But hold your horses...or rather, hold your puppies. You can't just jump into leash training. There's prep work involved. Your little furball has to get comfortable with wearing a collar or harness first. So, how do you get that done without causing a ruckus? I'm glad you asked!

First thing's first – the gear. A collar or harness isn't a one-size-fits-all affair. You've gotta find the right fit for your pup. Adjustable ones are the way to go. Your puppy's gonna grow and you don't want to be buying a new collar every month, right? And the leash? Pick something light, non-retractable. You need control, not a fishing expedition.

So, now you've got your equipment sorted. But don't just throw it onto your pup. Patience, my dear friend, patience. Let the little guy sniff it out first. Investigate. Get acquainted. Then, only when they're comfortable, gently put it on. Treat them with a soft pat or a yummy morsel. Let 'em wear it around the house, bit by bit. Extend the duration gradually. No rush.

Time to up the ante. Attach the leash to the comfy collar or harness. But don't start walking just yet. Let your pup roam around, leash trailing behind. Supervised, of course. This helps your pup to get used to the feel of the leash without the demands of walking on it just yet. It's all about taking baby steps to a well-behaved walk in the park.

Teaching Loose-Leash Walking

Step right up, pup parents! Today's masterclass is all about loose-leash walking. Now, what in tarnation is that, you ask? Well, it's when your pupper walks in step with you, neither yanking the leash nor dragging their paws. Picture it: a peaceful, pull-free stroll with your furry friend. Sounds dreamy, right? But it's gonna take some patience, consistency, and a sprinkle of know-how. Here's the game plan:

Step One: Start in the safety of your own home. Too many distractions could derail the training session. Keep the leash in one hand, and arm the other with treats or a clicker. Your puppy will quickly figure out this isn't just another game of tug-of-war.

Step Two: Cue the...cue. You need a signal that tells your puppy it's time to hit the road. "Heel", "let's go", "mush", anything that tickles your fancy. Just remember to stick with it. Consistency is key here.

Step Three: Reward the good behavior. When your pup sticks by your side, shower them with treats or praises. If they start leading the march, stop in your tracks. Wait for them to return to your side. Yanking the leash? No-no. That's only gonna scare them.

Step Four: Introduce twists and turns. Literally. Add turns and direction changes to your training repertoire. This teaches your pup to keep their eyes on you and follow your lead. Praises and treats go to those who ace this stage.

Step Five: Let's up the ante. Slowly introduce distractions to your training sessions. Other dogs, people, sounds – the works. But remember, start from afar and gradually get closer. The goal is to keep your puppy focused on you, not the squirrel running up the tree.

The Final Step: Keep at it. Patience, dear friend, patience. Your pup won't master loose-leash walking overnight. Keep your training consistent and give them time. They're learning an essential skill, after all.

And there you have it, folks! Six steps to blissful, relaxed walks with your doggo. It's a journey worth taking. Enjoy the ride, or in this case, the walk.

Clicker Training

Well, butter my biscuits! I've come across a treasure trove of puppy training wisdom, and it goes by the name of clicker training. This ain't no hocus-pocus, folks. It's a scientific method – a blend of positive re-inforcement and sound, to be precise – that'll get your puppy learning new tricks in no time. I reckon it's one of the fairest, kindest ways to teach a young'un new thing, and I urge y'all to give it a whirl.

What's clicker training? Well, it's a page outta the book of operant conditioning. In simpler words, it's teaching your pup to associate a behavior with a consequence – think rewards or penalties. A clicker, a nifty little device that fits in your palm, is the star of this show. It makes a unique sound, a clear "click," right when your pup does something right. The "click" is then followed by a treat, reinforcing the good behavior. It's pretty neat, if I do say so myself. The perks of clicker training? Clear as a bell communication for starters. That "click" tells your puppy they've done good, cutting out the guesswork. This can speed up the learning process, too. The clicker points out the exact behavior to reinforce, making training more efficient. And let's not forget, it's built on positive reinforcement, strengthening the bond between you and your little furball. Makes training a joy, rather than a chore. So, how do you get on this clicker training bandwagon? Here's your roadmap:

- **Kick-off with charging the clicker.** This ain't about batteries. You're making the click sound a positive signal. Simply click and follow it with a treat. Rinse and repeat until your pup's ears perk up with the sound of the click.

- **Next, capture a behavior.** Wait for your puppy to naturally do something you want (like sitting or lying down), then immediately click and treat. Patience is key here, folks. It'll take time, but it's worth it.

- **Got a complex behavior to teach?** Try shaping. Break the behavior down into small steps and reward each little progress. If roll-over is your goal, start by clicking and treating when they lie down, shift their weight, and so on until they complete a full roll.

- **Once your pup gets the hang of responding to the clicker, bring in a cue.** A hand signal or a verbal command will do. Say the cue, then click and treat. Gradually, your pup will respond to the cue alone, and you can phase out the clicker.

- **Finally, proof and generalize.** Practice the behavior in different places, with different lev- els of distractions. This makes sure your pup can perform the trick in any situation.

Teaching Key Commands

In this here chapter, we're delving into the nitty-gritty of raising a good boy or girl, who's not just the talk of the town but also knows their manners to a T. I'm talking about training your puppy to respond to key commands. It's a labor of love, patience, and time. But oh boy, is it worth it! So, ready to shape your ball of fluff into a model citizen? Great! I'm here to share practical examples and tips on teaching your puppy the ABCs of commands. With a good dose of consistency, a sprinkling of positive reinforcement, and a whole lotta love, you and your four-legged compadre are all set for a rewarding learning journey.

Respond to Name

The first step in our command-conquering journey is teaching your pup to respond to their name. Think of it as their personal catchy tune. It's the cornerstone for all the tricks they'll learn down the road. It's like ringing a bell that gets your puppy's attention, ensuring they're all ears and raring to learn.

1. First up, find a quiet spot. Somewhere free from distractions. It's all about making it easy for your furball to concentrate.

2. Then, let their name roll off your tongue. Say it out loud in a cheerful, energetic tone. Make it sound like the best thing since sliced bread.

3. The moment your puppy swivels their head your way, reward them. A treat, a pat, a word of praise - anything that makes their tail wag.

4. Lather, rinse, repeat. Do this multiple times a day. Once they've got the hang of it, slowly dial up the level of distractions.

5. And voila! You're on your way to having a puppy that perks up every time they hear their name. Isn't that a treat?

Come

This one is as vital as corn to a chicken. I'm talkin' about the "come" command. It's not just handy in a million different scenarios but also a lifeline to keep your pup safe. Strap in, because here's how you can teach your doggo this invaluable trick:

1. Firstly, park yourself a small stretch away from your little pup. Don't go far now, just enough to make this interesting for the both of you.

2. Now, call out their name and follow it up with a crisp "come". Make sure you're as clear and inviting as a sunny day in June.

3. Now wait for the magic. When your puppy trots over to you, let the praises rain down! Go ahead, shower them with a treat too.

4. Got it nailed down? Perfect. Now start turning up the difficulty dial. Increase the distance between you two, or introduce more distractions. But remember, slow and steady wins the race.

And there you have it! You've just taught your furry friend a command that's as essential as butter to cornbread.

Drop

Next up on our pupper command odyssey, we're saddling up for the "drop" command. Now, this ain't just a fancy trick for show and tell. It's darn important for nipping any budding possessive behavior in the bud, and keeping your puppy safe to boot. So, how 'bout we giddy up and learn this command? Follow these steps:

1. Hand over a toy or chew that your puppy is wild about. Let them sink their teeth into it, figuratively and literally.

2. Now comes the fun part. As your puppy enjoys their toy, wave a treat that would make their

tail wag faster than a rattlesnake's rattle. At the same time, say "drop" loud and clear.

3. Your puppy should let go of the toy like a hot potato to get the treat. Once they do, heap praises on them like they just won the grand rodeo.

4. Keep at it! Practice makes perfect, after all. As your puppy gets better at this, start using the command without the treat bait.

Sit

Buckle up, because we're about to learn the basics - the "sit" command. This is like teaching your puppy their ABCs, a cornerstone of good manners and self-control. With the right approach, you'll have your four-legged friend sitting on command faster than a greased lightning bolt.

1. Hold a treat close to your puppy's sniffer, then start moving it slowly up and back over their head, like a tasty, flying target.

2. It's like magic, I tell you! Your puppy's bottom will naturally drop into a sitting position as their head follows the treat's tantalizing trail.

3. The moment your pup's rear touches the ground, say "sit" in a clear voice. Make a fuss over them and give them the treat. They've earned it!

4. Rinse and repeat this process several times a day. And here's the kicker - slowly stop using the treat as a lure over time.

Wait

Next, we'll tackle the "wait" command. This little gem teaches your puppy to cool their jets and stay put. Great for reigning in impulsive behaviors and ensuring safety. So, without further ado, let's dive right in:

1. Get your puppy to sit first. Then, whip out a treat and hold it in front of them. As you do, say "wait" loud and clear.

2. Play the waiting game for a few seconds. Then, give them the green light with an "okay" and hand them the treat. They've earned it!

3. Now, this is where things get interesting. Start stretching out the waiting period and toss in some distractions. Remember, it's about building patience and focus, one step at a time.

4. Lastly, put the command to the test in different scenarios - waiting at the doorway before a walk, holding off before crossing the street, and so on. It's all about practical application, after all.

Watch

Now let's discuss the next command on our list, the "watch" command. This handy dandy command encourages your puppy to make eye contact with you. It's a fantastic way to keep your pup focused during training and it helps to reinforce the bond between the two of you.

1. Grab a treat and hold it near your peepers. As you do, say "watch" in a clear, firm voice.

2. Now wait for the magic to happen. The moment your puppy makes eye contact, give 'em a heap of praise and reward them with that treat. Good job, little buddy!

3. Now, we're not done just yet. Gradually extend the time they're making eye contact and slowly introduce some distractions. This is all about building up focus and patience.

4. Eventually, start using the command without a treat. Instead, reward your puppy with attention

and praise. After all, they're doing this for you, not for the snack!

Stay

Now, we're on to the mother of all puppy commands, the ever-important "stay." The "stay" command is your ticket to keeping a handle on your puppy in all sorts of scenarios. Plus, it teaches your pup a good measure of self-control and patience.

1. So, without further ado, let's jump right in:

2. First things first, have your puppy sit or lie down.

3. Next, extend your hand out with your palm facing your little companion and say "stay" in a clear, assertive voice.

4. Now comes the fun part. Take a few steps back, then return to your puppy. If they've stayed put like you asked, heap on the praise and give them a well-earned treat.

5. Once they've gotten the hang of it, start extending the distance and duration of the "stay" command. Remember to always reward your puppy for a job well done.

6. Last but not least, start throwing in some distractions and mix up the environments you practice in. Variety is the spice of life, after all.

Lie Down

Next up in the command center is the "lie down" command. Trust me, this one's a doozy! It's not only a great tool for keeping your puppy calm and composed in different scenarios, but it's also a pretty easy trick to teach your fluffy friend.

1. Start off by getting your puppy to sit. Got it? Fantastic.

2. Now, hold a treat close to their nose (but don't let them snatch it just yet) and gently lower it to the ground. As you do this, make sure to say "lie down" in a calm, clear voice.

3. Here's the fun part: as your puppy's head follows the treat, they'll naturally fold into a lying down position. It's like magic, I tell ya!

4. Once your puppy's lying down like a pro, shower them with praises and let them have the treat. They've earned it!

5. Now, rinse and repeat. Practice makes perfect, after all. Over time, you can gradually stop using the treat as bait.

Heel

The "heel" command - quite a hot ticket item in the dog-training world, isn't it? This one teaches your puppy to saunter by your side without tugging on the leash, making your outdoor strolls a breezy delight. Let's not delay and dive right in:

1. Kick things off with a treat in your hand - allow your puppy to get a good whiff of it. They're going to work for it after all!

2. Up next, tell your puppy "heel" and start walking. Make sure to hold the treat at your side, just a smidge above your puppy's head.

3. If your puppy does a good job following the treat and keeps close to your side, shower them with praise and give them the treat. Let them know they did well!

4. Once your puppy starts getting the hang of it, start to up the ante. Gradually increase the "heel"

command's duration and throw in some distractions to keep things challenging.

5. The end game? Practice this command during your walks and eventually, you won't need the treat anymore. Your praise and attention will be the ultimate reward for your puppy!

Decoding Your Dog's Body Language

The capacity to effectively communicate despite existing as different species remains one of the most captivating facets found within human-canine relationships. Fundamental within this particular form of interaction lies an extensive grasp on your dog's body language patterns. Thus, offering various expressions that afford a deepened understanding relating directly towards your puppy's emotional state-of-being as well as their determined intentions and requirements alike. Ergo acquiring adeptness when it comes to accurately interpreting these visual cues becomes an irreplaceable skillset for those wholly involved within any form relating directly towards puppy training initiatives.

Understanding Common Signals and Postures

Just as human body language communicates a variety of feelings and intentions, so does your dog's. While there are breed and individual variances, many aspects of canine body language are universal.

- **Tail Wagging:** Contrary to popular belief, tail wagging isn't always a sign of happiness. The position and movement of the tail can indicate a range of emotions. A high, stiff wag may sig- nal alertness or aggression, while a low and loosewag typically signifies relaxation or submission.

- **Ears:** A dog's ears can be expressive. Pricked, forward-facing ears suggest attentiveness or interest, whereas flattened ears may convey fear or submission.

- **Body Posture:** A relaxed, loose posture often indicates a comfortable, content dog. On the other hand, a stiff or lowered body can be a sign of fear, anxiety, or aggression.

- **Eyes:** Direct, prolonged eye contact from your dog might be a challenge or a display of dominance, while averting gaze can signal submission or discomfort. Dilated pupils often suggest excitement or fear.

Responding Appropriately to Your Dog's Cues

Recognizing your puppy's body language is just the first step. Responding appropriately to their cues is equally important in fostering effective communication and mutual understanding.

- **Positive Signals:** When your puppy shows signs of comfort and happiness (like a relaxed body and a gently wagging tail), reinforce this positive behavior. Continue whatever action led to this response, be it petting, playing, or simply being in their presence.

- **Fear or Anxiety:** If your puppy displays signs of fear or anxiety, like flattened ears, a tucked tail, or a crouched body, it's important to identify and address the source of their discomfort. Avoid forceful confrontation and instead opt for gentle reassurance. In some cases, it may be helpful to remove your puppy from the stressful situation entirely.

- **Aggression or Dominance:** Signs of aggression or dominance, such as stiff posture, bared teeth, or a high, stiff tail wag, require careful handling. It's crucial not to respond with aggression of your own. Instead, maintain calm and assert your leadership through firm, confident commands.

By taking the time to understand your puppy's body language and respond appropriately, you're ensuring a healthier, happier relationship with your pet. This mutual understanding not only deepens your bond but also makes training sessions more effective and enjoyable for both of you. Remember, every dog is unique, so while these general interpretations offer a starting point, getting to know your specific pet's behaviors is crucial to truly understand their communication.

HEALTH AND WELLBEING

"Dogs are wise. They crawl away into a quiet corner and lick their wounds and do not rejoin the world until they are whole once more."

—Agatha Christie

Imagine being in a world where you can't verbally express your needs, fears, or discomforts. A world where you entirely rely on others to interpret your subtle cues, meet your needs, and ensure your well-being. This is the world your dog inhabits. Therefore, understanding your puppy's perspective is the cornerstone of responsible and successful dog ownership.

Importance of Prioritizing the Dog's Welfare

Caring for a dog goes beyond the basics like food and shelter; it involves ensuring their overall well-being as living creatures with needs and emotions. Dogs have the capacity to feel various emotions such as happiness, sadness, fear, and love. Respecting these emotions greatly affects their psychological wellbeing prioritizing your four-legged companions' welfare directly impacts its quality of life, a well-cared for dog will maintain optimal physical health balance emotionally, and exhibit desirable behavior. Prioritizing your companion's welfare entails fulfilling both its physical necessities — such as nutrition, exercise, healthcare, and grooming — and its psychological ones, such as companionship, intellectual stimulation and feeling secure. Allow me take an instance of Bella, a Golden Retriever keen on company coupled with physical exercise. If her family fails to cater for this bonding and activity needs. She may resort to destructive tendencies like chewing furniture or excessive barking brought about by boredom or anxiety. It isn't that Bella is a 'bad dog', rather it simply implies that her fundamental requirements are overlooked.

Meeting Your Dog's Essential Needs

Just like humans have basic necessities that need to be fulfilled in order to lead healthy lives filled with happiness dogs too have fundamental requirements which need your attention. These requirements fall under three main categories: physiological needs, safety needs, and psychological needs. To ensure the well-being of our loyal friends. It is necessary then that we understand these necessities better. Physiological requirements encompass proper nutrition that is specific to your dogs' age, breed, and overall health status. Furthermore, keeping them physically fit through regular exercise diminishes the possibility of behavioral issues due to the excess energy. Never forget to provide them fresh, clean drinking water at all times.

Safety needs involve giving your precious fur baby regular visits to the veterinarian and making sure their vaccinations are up to date. This plays a crucial role in safeguarding them from diseases while simultaneously allowing you to detect any health concerns in their early stages. Also ensure that they have a safe and comfortable sleep space that promotes tranquility. Psychological demands are no less important than the others as our dogs are highly social creatures that require companionship. Quality time spent with your beloved pet along with mental stimulation through playtime activities like toys or training exercises greatly contribute towards their emotional well-being. Opportunities for play should also be provided for them. For instance, lets' consider Max - a Border Collie known for needing significant mental and physical stimulation. To meet these needs his family actively involves him in daily activities. These include providing him with puzzle toys as well as organizing frequent agility training sessions.

In order to effectively fulfil your furry companions essential necessities it becomes vital to understand their unique characteristics and preferences. By prioritizing their welfare. Demonstrating love, security, and fulfillment towards these incredible animals, you not only ensure good behavior but also forge a bond of friendship between you both.

Food and Nutrition

Your puppy relies heavily on food to thrive in various aspects of its life. Apart from facilitating its growth. It contributes to maintaining lustrous fur. Fortifying its immune system against illnesses and providing essential energy for its daily shenanigans. Nevertheless. Offering adequate nutrition entails more than simply placing a meal in front of your furry friend. It demands a comprehensive comprehension of its unique dietary requirements while carefully distinguishing between suitable and inappropriate nutrition options. Moreover, selecting appropriate rewards or treats becomes crucial during training sessions along with considering the potential benefits associated with homemade meals.

Essentials of Dog Nutrition

Similar to us humans, dogs require a well-balanced diet to ensure optimum health. However. The question arises: what consists of such a balanced diet for our canine companions? In essence it comprises proteins carbohydrates, fats, vitamins, and minerals each serving its own unique purpose. Proteins are of utmost importance for tissue repair and muscle growth especially during the crucial growing phase in puppies. While carbohydrates may not be vital. They do provide dogs with a valuable source of energy and assist in maintaining a healthy digestive system. Fats play an essential role by facilitating the absorption of certain vitamins and serving as an excellent energy source. Finally, vitamins and minerals are necessary for various metabolic reactions within the body. For instance, a growing Labrador pup named Ollie would greatly benefit from a protein rich diet that supports his rapid growth and high levels of energy.

Choosing the Right Dog Foods

With an overwhelming number of dog food brands to choose from. It can be a daunting task to select the right one. It is important to consider the standards set by the Association of American Feed Control Officials

(AAFCO) when making your decision. Look for a food label that indicates the product is complete and balanced ensuring that it contains all necessary nutrients. Additionally. Consider your dogs' life stage (puppy, adult, or senior) and size (small breed or large breed) when choosing their food. Different breeds have different nutritional requirements - for example. Yorkshire Terriers have different needs than Great Danes.

Understanding Toxic Foods

Although dogs can be overly enthusiastic about consuming anything they come across it is important to note that not all foods are safe for them. Several types of food can prove toxic to dogs, such as chocolate, grapes, raisins, onions, garlic, xylitol (a common sweetener). And alcohol. Hence it is crucial to ensure that these items are kept out of your dogs reach and that all members of your family comprehend the perils associated with these foods. In the unfortunate event of your dog ingesting any of these substances. It is highly advisable to promptly seek veterinary attention.

Choosing Suitable Rewards

Incorporating treats into your poppy's training sessions can serve as an excellent incentive; nevertheless.

It is vital to select appropriate ones. It is advisable for the treats to be small in order for your puppy not fill up too quickly and they must also promote their well-being by avoiding those high in sugar or artificial additives. Going for baby carrots, seedless apples, or a piece of boiled chicken usually satisfies many dogs' taste buds when it comes to rewards during training exercises. Nevertheless, keep in mind that these treats should only constitute roughly 10% of your beloved pets total daily caloric consumption.

Homemade Food Options and Precautions

Taking the time to prepare your dog's meals at home empowers you to have full control over what your furry friend is consuming. However. It is essential to recognize that doing so requires a solid comprehension of your dogs' specific nutritional requirements. Seeking guidance from a veterinary nutritionist will ensure that the diet you create for your dog is well balanced and tailored to their individual life stage and overall health status. It is important to keep in mind that certain foods are highly beneficial for dogs, such as lean meats, select fruits and vegetables. And whole grains. On the flip side. There are foods like avocado, raw bread dough. And those high in salt and spices that can pose potential risks or harm. The responsibility of managing your dog's dietary needs may initially seem overwhelming due to the numerous factors to consider. However, with the support of your veterinarian and an expanding understanding of what nourishes your pet best this challenge can ultimately lead to improved health and even extend their lifespan. Demonstrating love and care towards your canine companion has many forms of expression. With proper nutrition being just one vital aspect.

The Perfect Meal Plan

When you design a meal plan for your canine companion with utmost care, it can prove highly effective in ensuring they receive an optimally balanced diet that caters precisely to their unique requirements. Remember that these illustrations provided are solely meant as guidance; any alterations made to your pet's feeding routine must be approached with caution under the supervision of either a qualified veterinary nutritionist or veterinarian themselves. Your four-legged friend's specific breed classification, size, demographic age characteristics, body weight registers, breakdowns involving daily exertion levels, and current state of overall health – such aspects efficiently combine in a cumulative manner to ultimately determine what kind of dietary regimen they'd find best suited. Let us now peruse distinctive meal plans intended for three dissimilar types of dogs: an adult belonging to a smaller breed, a puppy from larger cur breeds, and finally an elderly senior dog grappling with aging issues.

1. Small Breed Adult Dog (For example: Chihuahua)

Adult small breeds have fast metabolisms and usually require a diet high in quality protein and fat.

Breakfast:
- 1/4 cup of high-quality small breed dry dog food
- A tablespoon of wet food (for added hydration and flavor)

Lunch:
- 1/4 cup of high-quality small breed dry dog food
- Dinner:
- 1/4 cup of high-quality small breed dry dog food
- A teaspoon of cooked lean chicken or turkey for added protein

Treats:
- Small dog-friendly veggies like carrot slices or green beans, used sparingly throughout the day during training or rewarding good behavior

2. Large Breed Puppy (For example: Labrador Retriever)

Large breed puppies like Labradors have specific dietary needs to support their rapid growth and prevent joint health issues later in life.

Breakfast:
- 1 cup of large breed puppy dry food
- A tablespoon of wet puppy food (for added hydration and flavor)

Lunch:
- 1 cup of large breed puppy dry food
- A few pieces of cooked vegetables like sweet potatoes or carrots

Dinner:
- 1 cup of large breed puppy dry food
- A tablespoon of wet puppy food
- A teaspoon of fish oil for added omega-3 and omega-6 fatty acids

Treats:
- Large breed puppy-specific treats used sparingly throughout the day during training or rewarding good behavior

3. Senior Dog (For example: German Shepherd)

Senior dogs may have decreased activity levels and potential health issues, such as arthritis or obesity, which necessitate a different diet.

Breakfast:
- 3/4 cup of senior-specific dry dog food
- A tablespoon of wet senior dog food for added hydration and flavor

Lunch:
- 1/4 cup of cooked lean protein (like chicken or turkey)

Dinner:
- 3/4 cup of senior-specific dry dog food
- A tablespoon of wet senior dog food
- A sprinkle of a joint supplement recommended by your vet, if necessary

Treats:
- Lower-calorie dog treats or dog-friendly veggies used sparingly throughout the day during training or rewarding good behavior

Please note: Always ensure your dog has access to fresh, clean water throughout the day. It's an essential part of their diet. Also, these meal plans are just starting points and the portions may need to be adjusted based on your dog's individual energy needs. Consult with your vet to ensure that your dog's meal plan meets their specific dietary requirements.

House Training

Successfully ensuring that your puppy or mature dog is well acclimated to their new home heavily relies on effective house training techniques. Though the path might prove arduous at times staying committed to this process with unwavering patience can lead to immense benefits. In doing so. You establish a peaceful abode where both you and your cherished canine partner can flourish together.

Basics of House Training

To effectively train your dog it is important to understand their needs and learn to anticipate their toilet habits. This involves being able to recognize the signs that indicate your dog needs to eliminate such as sniffing around circling, whining, or seeking your attention. Additionally, it is essential to familiarize yourself with your dog's natural schedule. In the case of puppies, they typically need to go outside immediately after waking up. After eating. And after engaging in active play. This means that you will need to make numerous trips outdoors throughout the day. Conversely older dogs can typically hold it for longer periods and may require fewer outings. For example. If you have just brought home a puppy, start by taking them out every hour or two. This not only helps prevent accidents but also gives them plenty of opportunities to succeed and earn praise.

Setting a Routine

When it comes to house training maintaining consistency is essential for success. It is advisable to stick with a regular feeding schedule and limit water consumption before bedtime so as not to promote accidents at night. Designating an outdoor area specifically for elimination can greatly assist this process - make it a habit of leading your dog there every time. By establishing such consistency. You help your dog comprehend where they should go when nature calls. For instance, Jareya Training Services explains that when training their puppy Bella dog owners should strive for consistent meal times followed by immediate trips outside. Furthermore, consistently bringing Bella to the same spot in the yard and using a trigger word such as "potty" can aid in reinforcing these associations.

Reinforcing Positive Behaviors

Positive reinforcement plays a crucial role in successfully house training your dog. Whenever your furry friend eliminates outdoors it is important to shower them with enthusiastic praise and a treat. This positive feedback sends a clear message to your dog that they have done something right motivating them to repeat the behavior in the future. For instance, if Bella starts going to the door when she needs to go out after consistent training for several days. This is a significant achievement that deserves celebration! Shower her with abundant praise and perhaps even offer her a special treat. However, if Bella happens to have an accident indoors. It is crucial not to scold or react negatively towards her. Instead, quietly clean up the mess and continue with the training routine. Remember, practicing patience is key when it comes to house training. Whether you are training a puppy or an older dog. It requires time and consistency. Nevertheless, in the end you will have a well-adjusted canine companion who brings joy into your home. It is important to understand that every dog is unique and some may require more time for house training than others do. Soar high with patience, understanding, and sprinkle it all with love along this journey of house training your beloved canine companion!

Prevention and Correction of Behavioral Issues

Now, take a knee, folks, let's talk some behavioral nitty-gritty in our four-legged buddies, shall we? Dogs, bless their hearts, are complex creatures filled with instincts that go way back, deeper than a bone bur- ied in the backyard. These quirks, these behaviors we might scrunch our brows at, they're often echoes of their ancient canine ancestors. So, yes, understanding these seemingly puzzling actions? It's a grand part of keeping your doggo happy and healthy. Think about it! That compulsive shoe chewing? The relentless tail chasing? These could just be Fido's way of saying, "Hey, I'm stressed!" or "I need more exercise!" Or, perhaps your furball's decided to do a spot-on impression of Houdini, escaping the backyard time and again. Frustrating? Absolutely. But remember, your canine buddy is not trying to ruin your day - they're just being, well, a dog!

Now, we're not about to throw our hands up and let Rover redecorate the living room with toilet paper. No, sir! The key here, the golden ticket, lies in addressing these behaviors positively and constructively. Rath- er than scolding, which can lead to a confused and scared pup, we need to guide them, help them chan- nel their canine energy in a way that keeps both your slippers and your sanity intact. Imagine this. Instead of shouting when Bruno nibbles your favorite loafers, offer him a dog-friendly chew toy. When Molly suddenly decides she's part greyhound and keeps sprinting across the yard, increase her exercise routine or consider doggy playdates. Get creative! Reward good behavior, guide them away from the not-so-good, and watch the magic unfold.

Keep in mind, this isn't an overnight fix. It's a journey, and like any good journey, it's packed with twists and turns. But, every step forward strengthens that bond between you and your fuzzy friend. Before you know it, you're less like an exasperated owner and more like a trusted guide, helping your pup navigate the maze of modern doggy life.

Remember, folks, we're all in this canine ballet together. Let's keep it positive, constructive, and filled with an abundance of tail wags. Balancing this equation? That's what makes a happy home for you and your beloved dog. Embrace the quirks, guide the paws, and enjoy the love-filled licks along the way.

- **Leash Pulling:** If your four-legged friend tends to relentlessly yank on their leash during walks, it can rapidly transform a delightful activity into a physically demanding task. The root cause behind this behavior lies in their sheer excitement and unquenchable urge for exploration. Thankfully, introducing positive reinforcement as a training technique proves incredibly fruitful in curbing this tendency effortlessly yet respectfully. Simply showering your beloved pooch with treats or heartfelt praise whenever they exhibit controlled walking behavior serves as powerful motivation to encourage them towards leashed composure and attentiveness.

- **Chewing:** Puppies engage in the act of chewing as a means to explore their environment and ease the discomfort caused by teething. On the other hand. Older dogs chew in order to maintain the strength of their jaws and ensure proper dental hygiene. It is essential to provide them with suitable chew toys and actively discourage them from chewing on unsuitable objects. If you happen to find your dog engaging in this inappropriate behavior gently interrupt them and offer a more suitable alternative for chewing.

- **Eating Poop:** The practice known as coprophagia or ingesting excrement could potentially disturb numerous individuals who happen to be dog owners. To dissuade such off-putting behavior from occurring within your canine companion's daily routine. It is vital that you prioritize maintaining an impeccably clean yard area. Additionally. Actively engaging your beloved pet in regular physical activities while simultaneously offering them a nourishing and balanced diet is highly advisable. However, if these attempts fail at mitigating the issue at hand and the behavior persistently prevails against all odds; consulting with a professional veterinary expert becomes crucial as they can help eliminate any potential underlying medical concerns that might contribute towards this vexing situation.

- **Jumping Up:** Frequently. Dogs exhibit exuberance by jumping up on individuals as a form of salutation or desire for attention. To effectively manage this behavior it is crucial to neglect your dogs' action of leaping up and provide rewards once they have all four paws planted securely on the ground. Furthermore, it would be appreciated if you could politely request visitors to adopt the same procedure.

- **Barking:** While barking is generally considered a common canine behavior, excessive barking calls for concern and necessitates specific interventions. It becomes crucial to comprehend why your dog might be incessantly barking as a first step towards addressing this issue effectively. By identifying the root cause appropriate training techniques like desensitization or counter conditioning can subsequently be implemented to tackle this matter respectfully and successfully.

- **Growling:** Growling is a means of communication that dogs employ to signal their discomfort, fear, or territorial instincts. It is crucial to refrain from punishing your dog for growling as it serves as their means of warning before resorting to potential biting. Instead, it is advisable to make an effort to identify and eliminate the cause of your dog's distress.

- **Play Biting:** Puppies engage in play biting as a natural part of their learning and socialization process. However. If your puppy bites you too hard during play. It is important to respond in a way that teaches them proper boundaries. One effective method is to let out a high-pitched yelp, which imitates the response they would receive from another puppy. By doing so you help them recognize that their bite was too forceful.

- **Begging:** In order to discourage begging it is advisable to refrain from feeding your dog food from the table. Prior to partaking in a meal ensure that your dog has been adequately fed. If need be. Consider training them to remain in a separate room during the time you are dining.

- **Not Listening:** To successfully teach your dog to respond to your commands. It is crucial to maintain consistency, patience. And utilize positive reinforcement. Begin by focusing on fundamental commands such as "sit" "stay" and "come" and gradually progress towards more advanced instructions.

- **Submissive, Excited, and Marking Peeing:** These behaviors are frequently associated with the emotional state or territorial instincts of the dog. To address submissive or excited peeing, it is advisable to reduce overly stimulating greetings or intimidating interactions. For marking, neutering or spaying often proves beneficial, in addition to maintaining a consistent house training routine.

- **Separation Anxiety:** When dogs experience separation anxiety. It can sometimes result in them engaging in destructive behavior. To address this issue a suggested approach is to slowly get your dog accustomed to being alone and keep your departures and arrivals as calm and understated as possible. If the anxiety continues despite these efforts. It may be beneficial to seek guidance from a professional trainer or behaviorist.

- **Aggression:** Aggression in dogs may arise from various underlying factors such as fear, territoriality, or resource guarding. This is a significant behavioral problem that requires the expertise of a professional to properly address. It is critical to ensure the safety of both the dog and the individuals in its vicinity.

- **Common Fears:** Loud Sounds, Being Left Alone, Certain People, Vacuum Cleaner, the Bathtub: Using desensitization and counter conditioning techniques can be a highly effective means of managing fears in dogs. The key is to gradually expose your furry friend to the source of their fear ensuring that the intensity of the exposure remains low and that it takes place in a controlled environment. By rewarding your dog for maintaining a sense of calm during these exposures you can create a positive association that will help them overcome their fears.

Understanding and addressing your dog's behavioral issues is crucial for both their wellbeing and your own. Seeking professional help for difficult cases ensures that you and your beloved pet can live together in harmony and happiness. Enhance your dog training journey with our exclusive "Well Behaved Companion Program" which provides you with the essential tools to effectively train your dog and overcome common challenges. Bid farewell to obstacles in pet parenting and embrace a joyful bond with your furry friend. Discover the secret to your dog's best behavior by scanning the provided QR code. Gaining access to start enhancing your companionship experience today.

As an independent author, your feedback means the world to me.

Would you mind leaving an honest review on Amazon? It helps

immensely and takes just a moment. Just scan the QR code or

copy/paste this url:

https://www.amazon.com/review/create-review/?asin=

B0CT5TK5JD

UNDERSTANDING DOG MENTAL HEALTH & STIMULATION

Identifying Your Dog's Mental Needs

You know your pup's quirks, their every yawn, wag, and woof. You can predict when they're ready to unleash a burst of energy around the backyard or when they're more inclined for some quality lap time. But do you know what makes their brain tick—or should we say, "tock?" Welcome to your insider's guide to decoding your dog's mental mojo!

First up: Recognize that each dog is a unique fur-sonality, crafted from a blend of breed traits and individual quirks. While some breeds are born strategists, designed for complex tasks like herding or tracking, others are social butterflies, thriving on companionship and interactive play. Knowing your dog's breed traits offers a helpful starting point, but it's vital to appreciate their unique individuality.

Here's a playbook to help you unlock the secrets of your dog's mental desires:

Watch and Learn: Pay close attention to your pup during various activities. Are they thrilled with puzzle toys but give a 'meh' response to a plain old game of fetch? That's your clue!

The Experimental Phase: Fear not! Dabble in a mix of activities, from basic to brain-busting. This book offers a buffet of mental exercises that span the spectrum from "Oh, this is child's play!" to "Wow, my dog's a genius!"

Expert Opinions Matter: If you're hitting a wall in pinpointing your dog's mental needs, consult a professional dog trainer or veterinary behaviorist. These experts can provide customized guidance to set you and your pup on a meaningful mental adventure.

Behavioral Barometer: Watch for signs like stress, apathy, or general boredom when introducing new activities. Tailor your approach based on these cues because, let's face it, if it's not fun for them, it won't be for you either.

The Family Council: Remember, insights can come from anyone who spends time with your dog. Sharing observations with family members can give you a 360-degree view of what mentally stimulates your pooch.

Whether your dog is a puzzler par excellence or the life of the doggy party, understanding their cognitive cravings is your first step towards a richer, more satisfying life for both of you. Imagine knowing whether your pup prefers brain-bending Sudoku or laid-back crosswords. Both are great; they just serve different mental needs.

By the time you turn the last page of this chapter, you'll be ready to craft a mental enrichment plan that's as tailor-made as your dog's unique set of paw prints, paving the way for a life filled with more wagging, less worrying, and a whole lot of happy moments.

Problem-Solving Games

Alright, fellow dog lovers, it's playtime—a very specific, strategically planned, and awesomely fun playtime that will send your pup's neurons firing like fireworks on New Year's Eve. Here are some hand-picked, vet-approved games to crank up the cognitive dial for your dogs.

Classic Kong and Frozen Treats

Instructions:
- Take a Kong toy and fill it with a blend of kibble and a dog-safe treat spread, like peanut butter (make sure it's xylitol-free).
- Freeze the Kong for a couple of hours.
- Once it's frozen, hand it over to your pooch and watch them get to work!

Tips:
- Experiment with different fillings like mashed banana, plain yogurt, or wet dog food.
- For the first few times, make it easier by not freezing it so your dog gets the hang of it.

Benefits:
- Mental stimulation as they figure out how to get the treats out.
- Sensory engagement with different textures and temperatures.
- Good for long-lasting engagement; buys you some quiet time!

Hide and Seek with a Twist

Instructions:
- Have family members hide in different parts of the house.

- Sit your dog and give the command "Find [Name]".
- When the dog finds them, the hider gives the dog a treat.

Tips:
- Start with just one hider initially, and increase complexity by adding more people or hiding spots.
- Use the "Stay" command to keep your dog in place while the hiders get into position.

Benefits:
- Enhances listening skills and obedience to commands.
- Boosts scent-tracking abilities.
- Encourages familial interaction, strengthening bonds.

Cup Shuffle Game

Instructions:
- Place three upside-down cups on the floor.
- Hide a treat under one of the cups.
- Shuffle the cups around.
- Ask your dog to find the treat with a "Find It" command.

Tips:
- Start with slow shuffles, then increase the speed as your dog gets better at the game.

- You can also increase the number of cups to up the challenge.

Benefits:
- Encourages focus and concentration.
- Develops problem-solving skills.
- Fun and interactive, good for indoor play.

Obstacle Course

Instructions:
- Set up an obstacle course using chairs, cones, or dog training equipment.
- Incorporate commands like "Over," "Under," "Through," and "Sit" at various stages.
- Guide your dog through the course, rewarding them as they successfully navigate through each command.

Tips:
- Always walk through the course first to show your dog what's expected.
- Keep it fun! Celebrate and reward, even if they don't get it perfectly right.

Benefits:
- Excellent for teaching new commands.
- Builds confidence and coordination.

- A physical workout that complements the mental stimulation.

Puzzle Boards and Mats

Instructions:
- Load treats or kibble into the different compartments of a dog puzzle board or snuffle mat.
- Place the puzzle or mat in front of your dog and encourage them to seek the treats.

Tips:
- Opt for puzzles that align with your dog's current skill level; don't make it too easy or too hard.
- Always supervise the first few sessions to make sure your dog doesn't chew or destroy the toy.

Benefits:
- Excellent for sniffing and foraging skills.
- Builds patience and persistence.
- Great for rainy days or quiet indoor play.

Sensory Engagement Activities

Your dog's world is a smorgasbord of smells, sights, and sounds, an ever-changing landscape of wonder that we, sadly, as humans, can only partially comprehend. Sensory engagement taps into this incredible world, adding layers of complexity and intrigue to your dog's daily life. So, shall we?

Scent Trails

Instructions:
- Take some dog-friendly essential oils or food extracts like lavender or vanilla and apply a few drops to a piece of fabric.
- Drag the fabric along the floor to create a scent trail leading to a hidden stash of treats.

Tips:
- Start with a short and simple trail and gradually make it longer and more complex.
- Always let your dog sniff the scent source first so they know what they're tracking.

Benefits:
- Boosts olfactory senses and tracking skills.
- Adds a treasure hunt element to your dog's routine.

Sound Stimulation with Toys

Instructions:
- Use a variety of toys that make different noises—squeaky toys, bells, crinkle toys.
- Play fetch or tug-of-war, making sure to engage the noise features of the toy.

Tips:
- Change the toys frequently to keep your dog interested.
- Use this as an opportunity to reinforce fetch or drop commands.

Benefits:
- Enhances auditory senses.
- Adds a new layer of excitement to familiar games.

Textured Walking Paths

Instructions:
- Create a small pathway in your backyard or living room using different materials like grass, gravel, carpet, and wood.
- Walk your dog over these different surfaces while giving them time to explore each one.

Tips:
- Monitor your dog's paws to ensure they're comfortable and not irritated by any surfaces.
- Use positive reinforcement to encourage exploration.

Benefits:
- Exposes your dog to different tactile sensations, enhancing their sense of touch.
- Great for younger dogs to build confidence in walking on varied terrains.

Taste Exploration

Instructions:
- Offer small amounts of dog-friendly fruits and vegetables like carrots, blueberries, and watermelon.
- Observe how your dog reacts to different tastes and textures.

Tips:
- Always check with your vet to confirm which foods are safe for your dog.
- Introduce new foods gradually to avoid digestive issues.

Benefits:
- Introduces new flavors and textures, engaging the sense of taste.
- Can lead to healthier snack options for your dog.

Color Cues

Instructions:
- Use toys or flashcards of different colors.
- Teach your dog to differentiate between them using commands like "Pick Blue" or "Find Red."

Tips:
- Dogs see blue and yellow better than red and green, so start with those.
- Be consistent with the color names you use to avoid confusion.

Benefits:
- Stimulates visual perception.
- Adds an educational element to playtime, strengthening memory and understanding.

Let's now venture into a realm where spontaneity meets strategy—Quick and Fun Mental Stimulation.

Quick and Fun Mental Stimulation

You've got a high-energy fur missile and just 15 minutes before your Zoom meeting starts. What to do? Don't fret! Sometimes, it's those tiny pockets of time that can serve as golden opportunities for quick yet effective mental stimulation. These activities are your go-to, tried-and-true, faster-than-you-can-say-"sit" ways to keep your pup engaged on a tight schedule.

Speed Commands

Instructions:
- Stand in front of your dog and quickly cycle through basic commands like "Sit," "Stand," "Paw," and "Lie Down."
- Reward immediately for each correct response.

Tips:
- Keep the treats small and easy to eat so that you can keep the pace quick.
- Use a cheerful, high-pitched voice to keep the energy levels up.

Benefits:
- Quick reinforcement of basic commands.
- Great for short bursts of focus and attention training.

The 'Which Hand' Game

Instructions:
- Place a treat in one of your closed fists.
- Present both fists to your dog and ask, "Which hand?"
- Open the hand they paw or nose at. If it's the one with the treat, they get to eat it.

Tips:
- If your dog struggles, make it easier by showing them the treat as you close your fist.
- You can also use toys instead of treats.

Benefits:
- Encourages scent discrimination and choice-making.
- Can be played anywhere, anytime.

Toss and Find

Instructions:
- Lightly toss a treat or toy into a grassy area while your dog is watching.
- Give the command "Find it!" and let them search for the item.

Tips:
- Use a high-contrast item that is easy for your dog to see.
- If your dog is struggling, help guide them to the general area.

Benefits:
- Incorporates both physical and mental exercise.
- Enhances scent and tracking abilities.

The Cup Game (Mini Version)

Instructions:
- Take two small cups and a treat.
- Show your dog the treat, then hide it under one of the cups.
- Shuffle the cups and ask your dog to find the treat.

Tips:
- Use clear cups for the first few rounds to give your dog the idea.
- Shuffle more quickly as they get the hang of it.

Benefits:
- Quick focus and problem-solving exercise.
- Easily set up in any room.

Quick Agility Drills

Instructions:
- Use furniture or specific rooms as 'stations.'
- Guide your dog from station to station, incorporating commands like "Over the couch," "Under the table," "Into the bedroom," etc.

Tips:
- Start with just two or three stations and gradually add more.
- Always reward at each station to keep the momentum.

Benefits:
- Fast-paced physical and mental stimulation.
- Great for rainy days when outdoor activities are limited.

ADVANCED MENTAL EXERCISES

So you've tried the basics, and your dog's now giving you that, "Really, is that all you got?" look. Well, prepare to wipe that smug grin off their furry face (lovingly, of course). These cognitive challenges are designed to test the limits of your dog's brain power, engaging them in complex problem-solving that takes mental stimulation to a whole new level.

Puzzle Toys Level-Up

Instructions:
- Purchase advanced dog puzzle toys that require multiple steps to solve.
- Fill them with treats and let your dog figure it out.

Tips:
- Gradually increase the difficulty level. Don't jump straight into the most complicated puzzle.
- Use high-value treats for these exercises to keep their interest piqued.

Benefits:
- Builds focus and determination.

– Excellent for self-entertainment when you can't engage directly.

The Name Game

Instructions:
– Begin by frequently referring to one of your dog's toys by a specific name during playtime, like "Fetch the BALL!"
– Once they associate that name with the toy, lay out multiple toys and ask them to fetch by name.

Tips:
– Be consistent with the names you use.
– Start with two toys and gradually expand the selection.

Benefits:
– Enhances memory and association skills.
– Builds vocabulary, believe it or not!

Obstacle Course with Commands

Instructions:
– Create an obstacle course incorporating hurdles, tunnels, and platforms.
– Guide your dog through it, but add in commands like "Sit" or "Lie Down" at different stations.

Tips:
- Use a leash initially to help guide them if needed.
- Keep your commands clear and your tone upbeat.

Benefits:
- Merges physical and mental challenges into one activity.
- Builds obedience, agility, and problem-solving skills.

Hide and Seek... with a Twist

Instructions:
- Ask your dog to sit and stay in one room.
- Go to another room and hide a treat, then call your dog to find you.
- Once they find you, ask them to go back and fetch a specific toy from the first room.

Tips:
- Use rooms that are not too cluttered to minimize distractions.
- Initially, let them see where you are hiding the treat for easier discovery.

Benefits:
- Engages multiple skills like scent tracking, recall, and object identification.
- Provides variety and complexity in a single game.

Time-based Treat Search

Instructions:
- Create a map of your house and mark spots where you will hide treats.
- Hide the treats and set a timer, challenging your dog to find them all before time runs out.

Tips:
- Use a countdown timer with a beeping sound that your dog can hear as a signal.
- Start with ample time and reduce it gradually as they get better.

Benefits:
- Adds urgency and excitement to the task.
- Enhances focus and decision-making under pressure.

There you have it, a series of activities to push your canine Einstein to their intellectual limits. The aim is to keep both you and your furry companion guessing, learning, and evolving.

After these, your dog will be ready for whatever mind-bending challenges you—or life—throws at them.

Is your tail wagging to proceed to the next section?

Advanced Problem-Solving Activities

By now, your dog is not just fetching the newspaper; they're probably analyzing the headlines. Jokes aside, problem-solving is the heart of mental stimulation. These activities build on foundational skills to challenge your dog's decision-making and critical thinking abilities. And let's be honest, who couldn't use a dog capable of solving some of life's more complex puzzles?

The Multi-Step Fetch

Instructions:
- Place one toy at the end of a hallway or across the room.
- Place another toy in an adjacent room.
- Instruct your dog to first fetch the toy from the hallway and then immediately guide them to fetch the second toy from the other room.

Tips:
- Initially, guide them to each toy to establish the sequence.
- Gradually increase the distance between the two toys.

Benefits:
- Fosters sequential thinking and memory.
- Involves more physical exercise than a simple fetch.

The Food Maze

Instructions:
- Create a simple maze using cardboard or furniture.
- Place food at various points and a high-value treat at the end.
- Release your dog at the start and let them figure out how to navigate to the treats.

Tips:
- Supervise the activity to ensure your dog doesn't start chewing on the maze.
- Make the maze more complex over time.

Benefits:
- Improves problem-solving and navigation skills.
- A fun way to feed your dog and make mealtime exciting.

The Shell Game with Commands

Instructions:
- Set up the classic shell game but before revealing

the treat, ask your dog to perform a trick or obey a command.
– Only upon successful completion, reveal the treat.

Tips:
– Use a command your dog already knows well to prevent frustration.
– Switch up the commands to keep your dog engaged.

Benefits:
– Enhances focus and self-control.
– Adds an extra layer of complexity to a familiar game.

The Detective Game

Instructions:
– Hide a toy somewhere in the house.
– Offer your dog a scent sample by letting them sniff another toy of the same kind.
– Encourage them to find the hidden toy based solely on scent.

Tips:
– Use a unique scent that is easily distinguishable for your dog.
– Praise them loudly and reward them once they find the toy.

Benefits:
- Engages advanced olfactory capabilities.
- Develops deductive reasoning skills.

Puzzle Feeder Scavenger Hunt

Instructions:
- Fill a puzzle feeder with treats and hide it somewhere in the house.
- Create a trail of clues or smaller treats leading up to it.

Tips:
- Make sure the hiding spot is safe and accessible to your dog.
- Use verbal cues like "Find it!" to excite and guide them.

Benefits:
- Encourages investigation and logical thinking.
- Makes mealtime an adventure, prolonging the eating process to aid digestion.
- And there you have it, activities designed to stretch your dog's problem-solving muscles to their very limits.

While you may not yet have a canine Sherlock Holmes on your hands, these activities will get you one paw closer. Ready to craft some brain-boosting toys? Let's keep trotting along!

Skill-Enhancing Games

If you've ever thought your dog could outsmart you in a game of wits, then this section is right up your alley—or should we say, your dog's lane?

Treat Search with Obstacles

Instructions:
- Secretly hide treats around a designated room.
- Place small obstacles like cushions or low stools in your dog's path.
- Cheer your dog on as they navigate these obstacles to find their hidden treasures.

Tips:
- Ensure the obstacles are stable and not a safety risk.
- Start simple and up the ante as your pooch masters the basics.

Benefits:
- Increases problem-solving skills.
- Works on agility and spatial awareness.

Command Chains

Instructions:
- Link together several commands that your dog knows well, such as "Sit," "Paw," and "Roll Over."
- Guide your dog to complete these actions in sequence, rewarding them with a treat at the end.

Tips:
- Begin with two to three commands and extend the chain as your dog gets more confident.
- Immediate rewards help reinforce the behavior.

Benefits:
- Builds memory and enhances sequential reasoning.
- Encourages obedience and sharpens listening skills.

Hide and Snif   f

Instructions:
- Ask someone to hold your dog or have them "Stay."

– Go hide in a different room and then call for your dog to come find you.
– Upon finding you, direct them to locate a hidden treat in the same space.

Tips:
– Use a safe, obstacle-free environment for this activity.
– Change your hiding spots to keep the game fresh and challenging.

Benefits:
– Refines scent tracking abilities.
– Fosters stronger human-dog bonding.

The Balancing Act

Instructions:
– While your dog is in a "Sit" or "Lie Down" position, place a treat on their paw.
– Ask them to wait until you give the cue to gobble it up.

Tips:
– Your dog should be calm and attentive before you start this exercise.
– Begin with just a few seconds and gradually extend the time as they become proficient.

Benefits:
- Encourages impulse control and patience.
- Helps with balance and focus.

There we have it! Skill-enhancing games that will make your dog the envy of the neighborhood—or at least the star pupil at the dog park. Ready for the next paw-some chapter? We're going to explore how you can DIY your own mentally stimulating toys. Get those crafting skills ready!

Tailoring for Size and Breed

Ah, the eternal question: Is size really everything? When it comes to mental stimulation for our furry family members, the answer is—sort of! Different breeds and sizes of dogs have distinct mental and physical attributes, and tailoring activities accordingly can spell the difference between a yawn and a tail-wagging good time.

Small Breeds: The Pint-Sized Geniuses

Instructions:
- For smaller breeds, consider puzzle toys that can be easily maneuvered.

- Use softer, smaller toys for tug-of-war games.

Tips:
- Small doesn't necessarily mean less energetic; tailor the difficulty level to your dog's enthusiasm.
- Use smaller treats as rewards to prevent overfeeding.

Benefits:
- Size-appropriate toys ensure safer play.
- Allows for breed-specific mental challenges, such as those that cater to a terrier's innate digging instincts.

Large Breeds: The Gentle Giants

Instructions:
- Opt for sturdy, larger puzzle toys that can withstand powerful jaws.
- Engage in outdoor mental exercises like treasure hunts that take advantage of their larger roaming range.

Tips:
- Large breeds often tire out more quickly, so balance mental and physical exercise carefully.
- Always check the durability of homemade toys, especially if your dog is a strong chewer.

Benefits:
- Activities tailored to size offer the right level of challenge, preventing boredom.
- Larger toys mean less risk of accidental swallowing.

Mixed Breeds: The Best of Both Worlds

Instructions:
- Assess your dog's specific traits and preferences. Is she more of a sprinter or a digger? A thinker or a chewer?
- Choose activities that highlight these unique characteristics.

Tips:
- Pay attention to stamina and interest levels during activities, adjusting as needed.
- Feel free to mix and match different exercises to keep things interesting.

Benefits:
- Catering to your mixed breed's specific traits can create a more enriching experience.
- Variety is the spice of life, and your mixed breed dog will thank you for a more dynamic routine.

Phew! We've covered quite a lot of ground, but this journey of discovery and enrichment isn't over yet. Up next, we're delving into real-life experiences to get a sense of how these strategies and exercises pan out in the world outside of this book. Ready for some heart-warming and enlightening case studies? Let's wag our way there!

THE 30-DAY MENTAL EXERCISE CALENDAR

How to Use This Calendar

Perform each daily task with your dog.

Feel free to swap days around to better suit your schedule, but try to follow the general progression.

You'll see that each week includes a "Review & Play" day to reinforce the activities you've worked on.

Week 1: The Basics

Day 1: Name Game
Instructions:
- Say your dog's name, and when they look at you, reward with a treat.

Benefits:
- Reinforces attention and responsiveness.

Day 2: Sit Command

Instructions:

- Ask your dog to sit before any fun activity: meals, walks, etc.

Benefits:

- Builds impulse control.

Day 3: Toy Identification

Instructions:

- Use the name of the toy while playing fetch. Repeat the name when they bring it back to you.

Benefits:

- Increases vocabulary and object recognition.

Day 4: Hide and Seek

Instructions:

- Ask your dog to sit and stay in a room.
- Go into another room and hide.
- Call out your dog's name or say "Come find me!"

Tips:

- If your dog struggles with the 'stay' command, you may need a second person to hold them briefly.
- Start with easy hiding spots and gradually make them more challenging.

Benefits:

- Enhances your dog's problem-solving skills.
- Strengthens the bond between you and your dog through interactive play.

Day 5: The Cup Game

Instructions:

– Place a treat under one of three cups.
– Shuffle the cups around while your dog watches.
– Encourage your dog to find the treat.

Tips:

– If your dog struggles, make the game easier by using fewer cups or not shuffling them.
– As your dog gets better, make it more challenging by adding more cups or shuffling them faster.

Benefits:

– Improves concentration and focus.
– Develops the ability to track moving objects.

Day 6: Fetch with a Twist

Instructions:

– Start a regular game of fetch.
– Intermittently ask your dog to 'sit' or 'stay' before you throw the toy.

Tips:

– Use high-value treats to reward compliance with the 'sit' or 'stay' command.
– Keep the session engaging; switch between different toys if your dog seems to lose interest.

Benefits:

– Improves impulse control and obedience during play.
– Adds a layer of mental challenge to a simple physical activity.

Day 7: Puzzle Feeder
Instructions:
- Fill a puzzle feeder with your dog's regular kibble or some healthy treats.
- Encourage your dog to interact with the feeder to get the food out.

Tips:
- Choose a puzzle feeder that is appropriate for your dog's size and skill level.
- Monitor your dog the first few times to ensure they're not getting frustrated or trying to break the toy.

Benefits:
- Stimulates your dog's brain as they work for their food.
- Can slow down their eating if they're a fast eater, aiding digestion.

Week 2: Slightly More Challenging

Day 8: Scent Trails
Instructions:
- Lay a trail of treats or kibble around your home or yard.
- Let your dog follow the trail to find the goodies.

Tips:

- Use low-calorie treats or break them into smaller pieces to manage your dog's weight.
- As your dog gets the hang of it, you can make the trails longer and more intricate.

Benefits:

- Stimulates your dog's sense of smell.
- Mimics natural foraging behavior.

Day 9: Name that Toy

Instructions:

- During playtime, consistently use a name for a particular toy like "ball" or "rope."
- After several sessions, test by asking your dog to fetch by name.

Tips:

- Start with only one or two toys to avoid overwhelming your dog.
- Use high-value rewards when your dog successfully fetches the correct toy.

Benefits:

- Teaches vocabulary and improves memory.
- Personalizes playtime, making it more engaging for your dog.

Day 10: Obstacle Course

Instructions:

- Set up a simple obstacle course using furniture, pillows, or specific dog-friendly structures.

- Lead your dog through it using treats or toys as motivation.

Tips:
- Make sure the obstacle course is safe and appropriate for your dog's size and agility level.
- Begin with a simple layout and increase complexity as your dog becomes more comfortable.

Benefits:
- Improves coordination and body awareness.
- Enhances your dog's confidence in navigating new environments.

Day 11: Which Hand?

Instructions:
- Hide a treat in one hand and present both closed fists to your dog.
- Let them sniff and paw to choose the hand with the treat.

Tips:
- If your dog seems confused, offer hints by slightly opening the correct fist.
- You can make it more challenging by switching hands faster.

Benefits:
- Encourages problem-solving.
- Enhances focus and impulse control.

Day 12: Toy Cleanup

Instructions:

– Teach your dog to pick up toys and place them in a designated box.

Tips:

– Use a clicker or verbal cue like "good" when your dog successfully places a toy in the box.
– Be patient, this may take several sessions.

Benefits:

– Fosters a sense of responsibility.
– Guess what? Your living room stays cleaner!

Day 13: Find the Treats in a Muffin Tin

Instructions:

– Place treats in some compartments of a muffin tin and cover all compartments with tennis balls.
– Encourage your dog to find the treats.

Tips:

– Use your dog's favorite treats to keep them interested.
– For more difficulty, tightly wedge the tennis balls into the compartments.

Benefits:

– Encourages multi-level problem-solving.
– Provides both mental and sensory stimulation.

Day 14: Balancing Act
Instructions:
- Ask your dog to 'sit' or 'lie down,' then place a treat on their paw or nose.
- Use a command like 'wait,' and then give them the treat after a few seconds.

Tips:
- Start with very short intervals and gradually increase the time.
- Use a clicker or verbal praise the moment your dog waits successfully.

Benefits:
- Enhances impulse control.
- Builds patience and focus.

Week 3: The Tail Never Lies!

Day 15: Spin the Bottle
Instructions:
- Take an empty plastic bottle and put some kibble or small treats inside.
- Encourage your dog to roll it around to dispense the treats.

Tips:
- Make sure to supervise playtime to ensure your dog doesn't chew the bottle.

- Use a small amount of kibble or treats to prevent overeating.

Benefits:
- Encourages independent play.
- Improves problem-solving skills.

Day 16: Sound Localization

Instructions:
- Make a noise behind your dog using a squeaky toy or your voice.
- Reward them when they turn toward the sound.

Tips:
- Start by making the noise close to them and gradually increase the distance.
- Use high-value treats to make it more rewarding.

Benefits:
- Sharpens listening and localization skills.
- Enhances focus and attention span.

Day 17: Cup Game

Instructions:
- Place a treat under one of three cups, then shuffle the cups around.
- Ask your dog to find the treat.

Tips:
- Start with slow movements so your dog can follow easily.
- As they get better, speed up the shuffling.

Benefits:
- Promotes logical thinking.
- Increases concentration.

Day 18: Interactive Feeders

Instructions:
- Use an interactive feeder or puzzle toy to feed your dog their regular meal.

Tips:
- Choose a feeder that is appropriate for your dog's size and skill level.
- Monitor your dog the first few times to ensure they understand how to get the food.

Benefits:
- Slows down eating, which is healthier for digestion.
- Provides mental stimulation during mealtime.

Day 19: Hidden Toy Search

Instructions:
- Hide your dog's favorite toy in a room and encourage them to find it.

Tips:
- Use vocal cues like "Find it!" to prompt your dog.
- Gradually make the hiding places more challenging.

Benefits:
- Increases scent-tracking abilities.
- Builds confidence.

Day 20: Roll Over and Play Dead

Instructions:

– Teach your dog the trick of rolling over or playing dead.

Tips:

– Use a clicker or a vocal cue to mark the behavior.
– Be patient, as this trick might require several short sessions.

Benefits:

– Builds body awareness and agility.
– Enhances the human-dog bond through advanced trick training.

Day 21: Mirror Game

Instructions:

– Mimic your dog's actions and encourage them to do the same.

Tips:

– Start with simple behaviors like sitting or lying down.
– Use treats or toys as rewards for successful mimicry.

Benefits:

– Encourages attention and focus.
– Enhances social learning abilities.

And there you have it—Week 3 is in the doggy bag! If your dog could high-five, I'm sure they'd be giving you one right now for all the fun and learning. Ready for the home stretch?

Absolutely, let's keep that tail wagging and the snout sniffing with the activities for Week 4!

Week 4: A Pawsome Finale!

Day 22: Agility Basics
Instructions:
- Create a simple agility course using furniture or special agility equipment.
- Guide your dog through the course using treats and vocal cues.

Tips:
- Start simple. A couple of jumps and a tunnel are a great beginning.
- Keep sessions short and positive to prevent overwhelm.

Benefits:
- Boosts physical and mental agility.
- Strengthens the bond between you and your dog.

Day 23: Scent Discrimination
Instructions:
- Line up several objects and scent one with a treat or a scent spray.

- Encourage your dog to find the scented object among the others.

Tips:
- Use objects with different textures and materials.
- Reward immediately when your dog finds the correct object.

Benefits:
- Enhances scent detection skills.
- Promotes cognitive engagement.

Day 24: Tug-of-Heart

Instructions:
- Engage in a good old game of tug using a safe tug toy.
- Incorporate commands like "drop it" and "take it" during the game.

Tips:
- Choose a tug toy that is easy on your dog's teeth.
- Make sure to let your dog win sometimes; it's a great confidence booster!

Benefits:
- Physical and mental exercise rolled into one.
- Reinforces obedience commands during playtime.

Day 25: Muffin Tin Magic

Instructions:
- Place treats or kibble in the cups of a muffin tin.
- Cover each cup with a tennis ball or small toy.
- Encourage your dog to find the treats.

Tips:
- Supervise to ensure your dog doesn't chew the muffin tin.
- Mix in some high-value treats among the kibble for an added challenge.

Benefits:
- Encourages problem-solving.
- Provides sensory enrichment through sniffing and pawing.

Day 26: Obstacle Course

Instructions:
- Set up an indoor obstacle course using pillows, boxes, and furniture.
- Use commands and treats to guide your dog through the course.

Tips:
- Keep the course simple at first, then gradually make it more complex.
- Always prioritize safety when setting up obstacles.

Benefits:
- Enhances coordination and physical agility.
- Builds confidence and trust.

Day 27: Trick for a Treat

Instructions:
- Teach your dog a brand-new trick, such as "spin," "wave," or "crawl."

Tips:

- Use a clicker or verbal marker to reinforce the desired behavior.
- Keep training sessions short and sweet, filled with treats and praise.

Benefits:
- Expands your dog's repertoire of tricks.
- Enhances focus and learning capabilities.

Day 28: Free Play

Instructions:
- Allow your dog some unstructured playtime, either with you or other dogs.

Tips:
- Monitor interactions to ensure play remains safe and positive.
- Use this time to observe what activities your dog naturally enjoys.

Benefits:
- Provides physical and mental release.
- Enhances social skills and happiness.

Congratulations! You've completed the 4-week journey of mental and sensory enrichment. Give yourself and your fur-baby some well-deserved belly rubs!

And that, dear reader, brings us to the end of this guide—but remember, it's just the beginning of a life filled with wagging tails, happy woofs, and a mentally enriched pup who is also your best friend.

CONCLUSION

Ah, dear reader! As we journey together, towards the end of our adventure into the world of puppy training, let us pause for a moment. Let us ponder upon the footprints of knowledge we have embedded along this trail. We've not only explored the responsibility of dog ownership, but also peered into the depth of companionship that lies within this task. It's not been merely an excursion, but a transformation.

If we roll back the scroll to our initial chapters, you'll recall how we delved into creating the ideal environment for our four-legged friends. We explored expert advice to make our homes accommodating for these furry beings, enriching their lives and our own.

As we ventured forth, we unraveled the intriguing world of dog training. Guided by principles and techniques, we dove into the exhilarating, and sometimes challenging, task of teaching tricks to our canine companions. In this realm, a metamorphosis occurs. Our bond with our furry friends deepens, we communicate better, and we find joy in the smallest of achievements. The whistles, the games of fetch, the mirth - all part of a tapestry woven with understanding, patience, and a healthy dose of fun.

Yet, amid this excitement, we never lost sight of the most significant aspect of dog ownership - the unconditional love it demands. The hardships of training are but pebbles in the path when faced with the overwhelming love these creatures inspire in us. We, as their guardians, ought to mirror the steadfast dedication they show us, for they hold parts of our hearts, reflecting our commitment in their trusting eyes.

As we gaze into the future of our journey, armed with the knowledge we've gained so far, we prepare to tread further. The guidance we have shared in these pages is not only about the practical aspects of dog ownership but also about the joy, companionship, and profound emotional bond it brings to our lives. Dogs, in their own way, bring enrichment to our lives through exercise, mental stimulation, and most importantly, love. And teaching them, in turn, enriches their lives.

So, dear reader, as we continue this beautiful journey, remember to treasure every moment. It is the privilege of caring for another living being, a beautiful creature who brings warmth, happiness, and unconditional love into our lives. Relish every second of this gift, for it creates a bond like no other, filled with lasting memories and cherished experiences.

Good luck, and cherish the journey,

Charlotte Marley

UNLOCK YOUR AMAZING BONUS!

SCAN THE QR CODE

OR

COPY AND PASTE THE URL:

https://free-bonus-amz.aweb.page/p/fe9bf1a3-410d-44a7-b333-5e985f00c785

As an independent author, your feedback means the world to me

Would you mind leaving an honest review on Amazon? It helps

immensely and takes just a moment. Just scan the QR code or

copy/paste this url:

https://www.amazon.com/review/create-review/?asin= B0CT5TK5JD

Made in the USA
Columbia, SC
04 October 2024